# Our Fortunes

ALSO BY JULIE KALENDEK:

*The Fundamental Difference*, Burning Deck, 1991
(trans.) *A Lesson in Music* by Jean Daive, Burning Deck, 1992

Julie Kalendek

# Our Fortunes

Burning Deck, Providence
2003

ACKNOWLEDGMENTS:

A French translation by Juliette Valéry and others was published as *Quand la vie se fait division* (Tours: Farrago, 1999).

The publication of this book was made possible, in part, by a grant from the Greenwall Fund of The Academy of American Poets.

Burning Deck Press is the Literature Program of ANYART: CONTEMPORARY ARTS CENTER, a tax-exempt (501c3), non-profit organization.

Cover by Keith Waldrop

# OUR FORTUNES

# Contents

# RETRACTION

The language, which grew too much inward
was supplanted by a vocabulary of custom.
The transparent gift of roses.
An ornate dance of obscure origin.
The finely hand-wrought chain.
Perhaps strenuous in conception,
but a sometimes delicate relief.

Had we stopped the words
before their engagement as weapons
in a civilization of machinery,
had we reflected to some degree—
was it better to have a man
look up to you or down your shirt,
look down on you or up your skirt?

And there is violence in accountability,
there are checkered feelings.
Days like weeks and weeks like hours.
Small yet visible jerks of pleasure.
Where to place the hands so as not
to harm the form. Movements of the tongue
which once aided speech.
No one defined those acts.
No one thought to subtract
an absence of fidelity.

Our choices are laid out in rows.
What a surprise when the woman declines
and is vicious, but reclined
at the appropriate angle.
As if she were taking gifts
and knowing it. As if strength
were never a response to brutality.

One other confidential discourse—
what made me assume an exchange?
My work on your behalf
comprises an addiction.
And though you take great pains
to spend toward your need,
it is a woman I would take like a child
in my arms, it is a child's disobedience
confused with an impulse to console.

It is a cycle of release.
It is fatigue coupled with distraction
that raises a screen against
the minuscule facts of desire.
Men will multiply to fill the space.
Men will vacillate.
It is an irony cultivated entirely
in the deep grasses
forgotten among the blades
where what can only crawl
is invisible and increasing.
As so many stones make sense
having broken from the earth.

A chemical flavored courtship
foretells intrusive ways.
A heart which serves these primitive conventions
must vary with space.

# Make

As we seem to begin
a Victorian privacy
persuades me.
I prowl the edges
of the scene.
I read the poems
of a beautiful woman.
She is a god at love.
I drink till I am sick.
I cannot find myself there.
When she really did go blind
he married her.
I consider the geography
of your need.

As we seem to begin
a vague repeating
is the highest form of order
I am capable of seeing.
You are fascinated by my
least favorite part.
I bleed the next morning
with gratitude
for such poised comprehension.
A chord strikes me
to distraction.
My better is not mine.
Time forces this hunger
for the indiscreet and

As we seem to begin
my attraction proves
flawed by conceit.
I am bound to disagree.
The heroine is introduced
to shame me with
her impeccable pedigree.
She comes between the pen
the page and the sheets.
My scrawl cannot elucidate
this incidental mixture
or fix a point
beyond the cure
of contact.

As we seem to begin
it's the end of a year
and no particular
day of the week.
I can't arouse a single hope
from the impure line.
I study the bruise
you left in the dark.
The shape is a sound
is an island
is a start
of release.
And word can prevent nothing
hung from the framework of belief.

# Our Fortunes

# 1.

He is made of earth
but very fine to be made first
and names each conquered creature
in our home


His index is invisible
as forest in the fog
tree by tree he maps me
his legend camouflaged


Did he mistake the day I came
Did he forget the clock
Did he mistake the sun's advance
or gauge this distance wrong

# 2.

When the earth did not revolve
when it was flat
and stationary in the universe


in the garden of plants unnamed


You would be on one side of the mountain
and I would be on the other


we live quietly on a lonely road


grow slowly within your fence of stone

# 3.

I sweep and wash and open shades
I pick up every mess we make
The dishes we dirty and then clean, the sheets


I change from white to green when spring comes


and I invite him in
but I don't think
these hands can capture him

# 4.

I glue our fortunes to the shelf above the sink
those written in red dissolve and bleed
those printed in black seem permanent ink


I faked a lesson
taught you verbs


we conjugate quite fair


Could I extract the message
if it wasn't really there

# 5.

a lady
heartily cast down


a man to make sons


a swale
aflood


palustris


sheen of water
pull of mud

# 6.

refrain the rain the ground is drowned

up river's mouth

Is cataract catastrophe
or placid as a wave within
troubled as the shrinking ice
at winter's end, at water's edge

drop of the sea, comfort me

# 7.

He staves off the horizon
He shoulders for a view


plows precarious
plateaus to the shore


is loud upon the mountain


and he sent forth a raven,
which went forth to and fro,
until the waters were dried up
from off the earth

## 8.

Sunday comes to quell
with time to tend
to microscopic worlds


seeds that might try to root in you


function precedes form


as I am of two heads
no cotyledon

# 9.

then autonomous recognition
precognition
mutual fright


an ear to each other's troubles
breeds out a witness
I require a love to make me careless


there will be only one night
in this little girl's life


so form my memories glacially
and round my thoughts be ice


may words comply
might action agree

# 10.

For desire conspires
not from heat


a spot in her cheek


the unworked soil
pressed and pure beneath
by time and pacing
and a roof that leaks

# 11.

he was sitting on one side of me and he was sitting on the other


I fabricate from season's foliage
I sort each fruit according to its kind


the female a modification preordained in the interest of reproduction


all flesh is grass
bent by wind
and blind preoccupation

# 12.

for temptation rules
all gravity, tides and floods
and in its rush will wash away
our previous purposes
our wasting days


I plan to read the paper fortunes
lost to weather
sunlight, water
matter passed from
form to form


and somewhere in the middle is the surface of no strain


no plain not followed by a slope


point a dazzled eye to this diminish

# 13.

I hatched a jealousy


I rationed need for you


breast apart from my heart


and so alike a formless tale
to empty line by line
in broken limbs and trails
and snaking vines


I have no garden of my own I propagate

# 14.

that which enters the body through the ear


that which can suspend itself
which presses against
that which dwells near


that which attenuates sharply
that which is heavy with bark
that which is hollowed out
which varies in form
and bears spines


that which pertains to curtains or veils
which is more than once divided


that which is with a venom fortified

# 15.

were we bad she excavated
while we slept
such a dream of cleaving
a clandestine meeting

of moving earth from deep within
of mysterious molten things
most elemental

she scraped the walls thin
she settled down to prove a lowering in
replete and yet devoid
so large and yet so thin

a structure bared
an ark without its skin

# 16.

as painful as a crooked pin
embedded in a silken thing


as sorry as the sinless


embarked upon
reverse the course
somnambulist that rows
trip to there
a pole a star


isolationist explorer and engineer
a foreign guest provoking stares


God saw it all
suffered invention unaware

# 17.

We decorate with life
the carbon of all things


it progresses like a painting
our colors blaze and cool


I bring things in to captivate
I stock the shelves with clever tools


and yet a higher hand arranges
them according to their use

# 18.

We mark these trees
as field succumbs to forest


Squirrels drop nuts
and plan for future transits


She whispered to him while he slept
as if to poison him

# 19.

oracles on a whim


not cleared to dream
while propped on pillows
I wreak and shriek


the corner of a Roman wall
a spiritless pyramid, a broad promenade
a splendid monument to mark your name


(in a closed church, one forgotten candle)


some victories we are not equipped to handle

## 20.

calibrate
my circus to your
cavalcade


a modern woman
does without
the carriage trade


for love is ever wrought
from inconvenience


And who will pay for this delay?
The nature of devotion
requires a diligent display

# 21.

You request a clock elastic


I purchase you a parcel of each day
and my bitter ministrations
which clang at oddest hours


and my exercise to drive
your grammar wild


makes the tears dry in my head


the long dark days
I work, you stay
in bed

## 22.


You lost the landscape deluxe
and man I am
too tired to feed you


Is thy bread more stale? Outside is not as far as you imagine

# 23.

dawn drags to dusk
you'll be gone a week
I can paint a room


Redecorate?


with me by his side he doesn't have to think
about me


forget Eve?


Remember, we are still
allowed to dream

24.

but obliged his rest
not to disturb
beholden to his mind
I not partake in haste


deter my urge to fly and
climb and twist upon his soul
with frequent repetitions
admonitions


what attraction at what cardinal point
flower
and first insect


the savages all do the same things, and each savage does everything

# 25.

a seed, a length of root
a part of heart
the smallest increment of care


a static ringing
a burst of singing
in our dirty ears


as life takes to division


To be nourished by revision


and the Lord shut him in

## 26.

he handles roughly
each piece


weighs what he may be
taking to the grave


walks on acres
some have never seen


an orchard, strange
with fruit, tree by tree

This book was designed and computer typeset in 10 pt. Palatino with Phyllis initials by Rosmarie Waldrop. Printed on 55 lb. Writers' Natural (an acid-free paper), smyth-sewn and glued into paper covers by McNaughton & Gunn in Saline, Michigan. The cover is by Keith Waldrop. There are 750 copies, of which 50 are numbered and signed by the author.